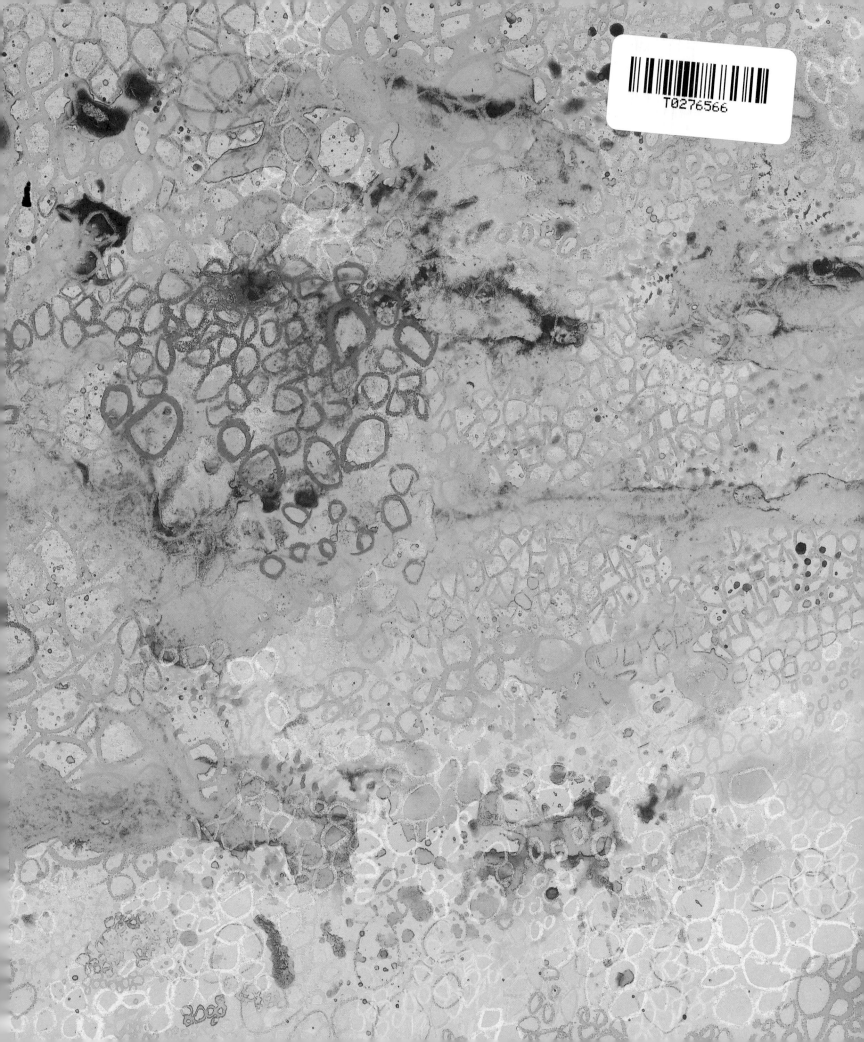

For Luca in Rome and thanks to everyone who is also enjoying this series.
Time to dive into dinosaurs!—C.B.

For Dan and Alfie.—S.W.

For my children's grandparents and Auntie Nic Nic. Thank you for helping
me carve out some time to work on this fantastic series.—A.H.

Text © 2024 Catherine Barr and Steve Williams.
Illustrations © 2024 Amy Husband.

First published in 2024 by Frances Lincoln Children's Books, an imprint of The Quarto Group.
100 Cummings Center, Suite 265D, Beverly, MA 01915, USA.
T (978) 282-9590 F (978) 283-2742 www.Quarto.com

A CIP record for this book is available from the Library of Congress.

ISBN: 978-0-7112-9088-4

The illustrations were created using watercolors, acrylics, collage, and pencils.
Set in Gill Sans.

Designer: Holly Jolley and Lyli Feng
Editor: Lotte Dobson
Production Controller: Dawn Cameron
Senior Commissioning Editor: Claire Grace
Art Director: Karissa Santos
Publisher: Peter Marley

Manufactured in Guangdong, China TT052024
10 9 8 7 6 5 4 3 2 1

MIX
Paper | Supporting
responsible forestry
FSC
www.fsc.org FSC® C016973

THE STORY OF
DINOSAURS

A first book about prehistoric beasts

Catherine Barr and **Steve Williams**
Illustrated by **Amy Husband**

Frances Lincoln
Children's Books

There have been five major mass
extinctions on planet Earth.
But the Great Dying has, so far, been the
biggest of all. It almost wiped out all
living things.

THE GREAT DYING
251 million years ago

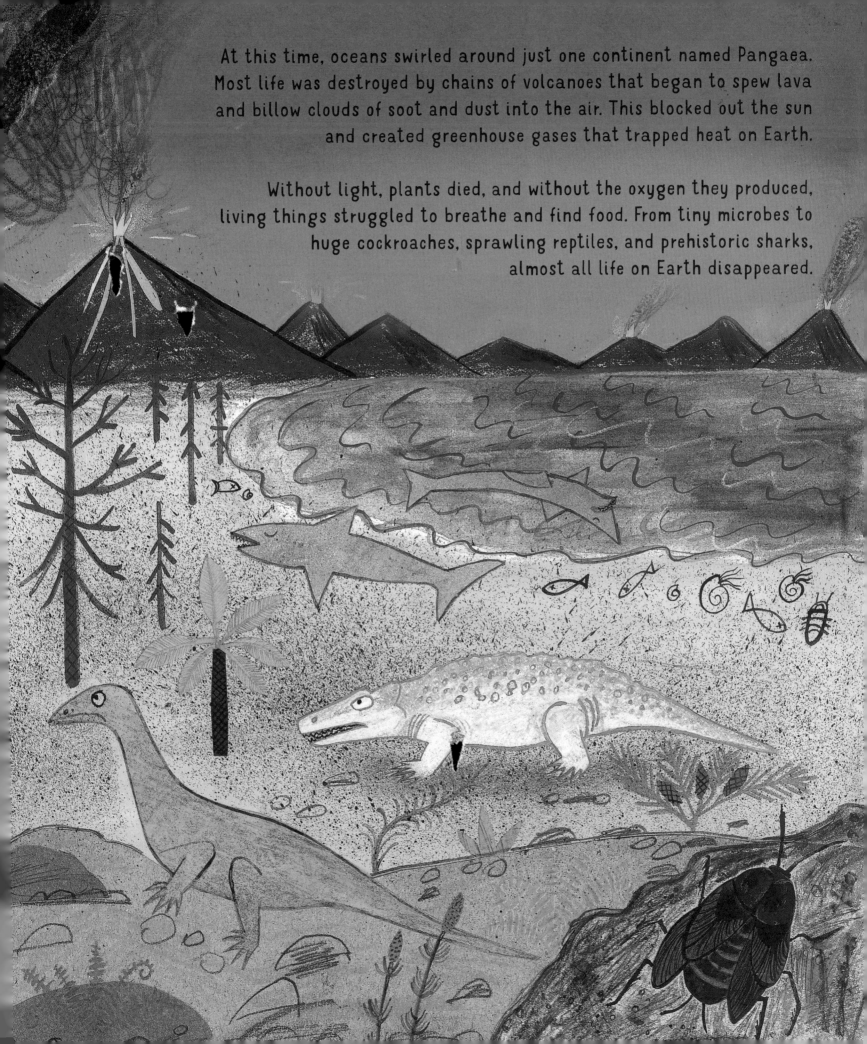

At this time, oceans swirled around just one continent named Pangaea. Most life was destroyed by chains of volcanoes that began to spew lava and billow clouds of soot and dust into the air. This blocked out the sun and created greenhouse gases that trapped heat on Earth.

Without light, plants died, and without the oxygen they produced, living things struggled to breathe and find food. From tiny microbes to huge cockroaches, sprawling reptiles, and prehistoric sharks, almost all life on Earth disappeared.

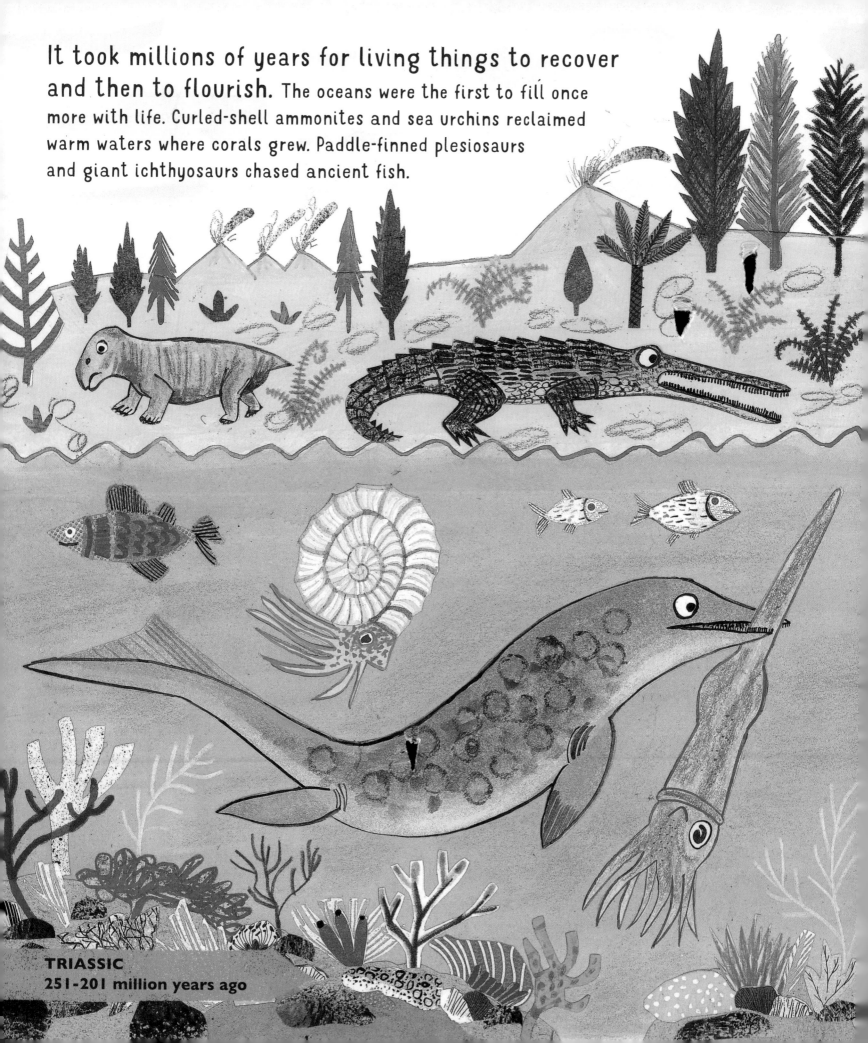

It took millions of years for living things to recover and then to flourish. The oceans were the first to fill once more with life. Curled-shell ammonites and sea urchins reclaimed warm waters where corals grew. Paddle-finned plesiosaurs and giant ichthyosaurs chased ancient fish.

TRIASSIC
251-201 million years ago

On land, crocodile-like creatures ruled. Some waddled through forests, while others chased prey on long legs. They were all predators on patrol.

There were other survivors too. Fox-sized reptiles raced around on two legs, instead of four. These upright meat-eaters were the first dinosaurs. As they evolved, they began to challenge the rule of other creatures. It was the Dawn of the Dinosaurs.

Toward the end of the Triassic, Pangaea began to crack. Over millions of years, this giant continent slowly split in two. On the separated continents of Gondwana and Laurasia, living things adapted to new habitats, and many more kinds of life evolved.

The dinosaurs wandering through ancient forests grew bigger. At first, they only ate meat, but over time, some dinosaur species evolved to eat plants too.

TRIASSIC
251–201 million years ago

These plant-eaters gathered in numbers as they began to grow in size. With longer necks, some dinosaurs called sauropods could reach higher branches. They saved energy just by standing still to eat.

While sauropods stretched up to nibble, beneath their feet, the planet's surface began to shift.

New landscapes were created by rock pushed upward into mountains. Land masses moved apart and seawater flooded between these smaller continents. Ocean winds now swept rain across inland deserts.

JURASSIC early
201-174 million years ago

Different species of dinosaurs evolved over time—each one specially adapted to survive. From speedy little plant-eaters to armor-plated giants, these vegetarian dinosaurs munched through the Jurassic's humid forests.

But where plant-eaters wandered, fearsome predators lurked. Huge meat-eating dinosaurs called theropods tore down prey with three sharp, curved claws. They left clues of these meaty meals behind in their poop!

There was safety in numbers so sauropods gathered in huge herds to go on long journeys. These super-giants stomped hundreds of miles in search of plants to eat. They swallowed small stones that helped them digest their tough planty diet.

JURASSIC late
164-145 million years ago

Other creatures felt the presence of these enormous dinosaurs. Beneath them, small mammals scuttled to escape their huge feet. Behind them, predators were wary of their tails whipping with a deadly strike. And above them, the world's first bird, Archaeopteryx, took flight from the trees.

In the Cretaceous period, land masses divided into the seven continents that we see on Earth today. Biodiversity boomed as living things adapted to the different climates and habitats on the separated lands.

The best-adapted dinosaurs survived in each environment. They developed wings, horns, spines, short arms, and duck-bills. Some even evolved colorful skin, ginger head crests, and sparkly iridescent feathers. It was an explosion of dinosaur diversity!

CRETACEOUS
145-66 million years ago

Landscapes also began to flood with color, as flowering plants spread. Bees, wasps, ants, and beetles clambered across forests where sauropod giants called titanosaurs grazed.

Argentinosaurus weighed as much as 14 elephants!

The titanosaurs were the biggest type of dinosaurs—their size is almost impossible to imagine! They had hollow bones and holes in their skulls, which made them less heavy. Like all dinosaurs, they also had special lungs that could absorb oxygen when they breathed in AND out, giving them enough energy to power their huge bodies.

A titanosaur called Argentinosaurus strode on strong pillar-like legs, eating endlessly to fill its big belly. These dinosaurs were some of the biggest animals to ever live on Earth.

Today's birds breathe like dinosaurs did.

CRETACEOUS
145-66 million years ago

Some of the most terrifying predators walked Earth during the Cretaceous. Velociraptor, which means "speedy thieves," were smart and aggressive hunters. Under the cover of darkness, they tracked down smaller dinosaurs, lizards, and mammals with their amazing sense of smell.

They ambushed and attacked, pinning their prey down with a strange and special claw.

CRETACEOUS
145–66 million years ago

But Velociraptor had a gentle side too. They were caring parents. Unlike sauropods, who laid their eggs and moved on, Velociraptor stuck around, made nests, and took care of their young.

Dinosaur young looked like miniature versions of their parents. They had to grow fast to live in a prehistoric world of hungry, bigger dinosaurs.

Fluffy Tyrannosaurus rex babies were no exception. They grew into fierce hunters in order to survive. As they grew, their fluff disappeared, and behind thin lips, they developed sharp teeth that could slice up prey or scavenge and steal another dinosaur's meal.

CRETACEOUS
145-66 million years ago

Tyrannosaurus rex's back legs grew powerful enough to hold up its giant body. Its stubby tail grew to balance the weight of its enormous head. Only its arms stayed small, but even these super-short limbs could grip prey in a deadly hold.

Dinosaurs even wandered across Antarctica. This southern continent was not the icy landscape we know today—in the Cretaceous it was covered in lush, swampy forests.

In winter, meat-eaters such as Imperobator splashed around in the dark. There is no sun in Antarctica for months of the year, so dinosaurs used night-vision to survive.

CRETACEOUS
145-66 million years ago

Dark polar winters were cold, and Antarctica's meat-eating dinosaurs had fluffy plumage that kept them warm. Fossils have revealed some dinosaurs had feathers that were colored, striped, or glittery under the sun.

Then, without warning, an asteroid struck, and planet Earth changed again.

This fast-traveling, gigantic space rock crashed into the sea. Its impact set off towering tidal waves, caused volcanoes to belch poisonous gases, and started a heatwave that sparked fires across the land. Dust and debris billowed up into the air and blocked out almost all sunlight.

ASTEROID
66 million years ago

For some time, our planet spun in near darkness. Without sunlight, plant life died and ecosystems collapsed. The great dinosaurs struggled and starved. Most life on Earth disappeared again.

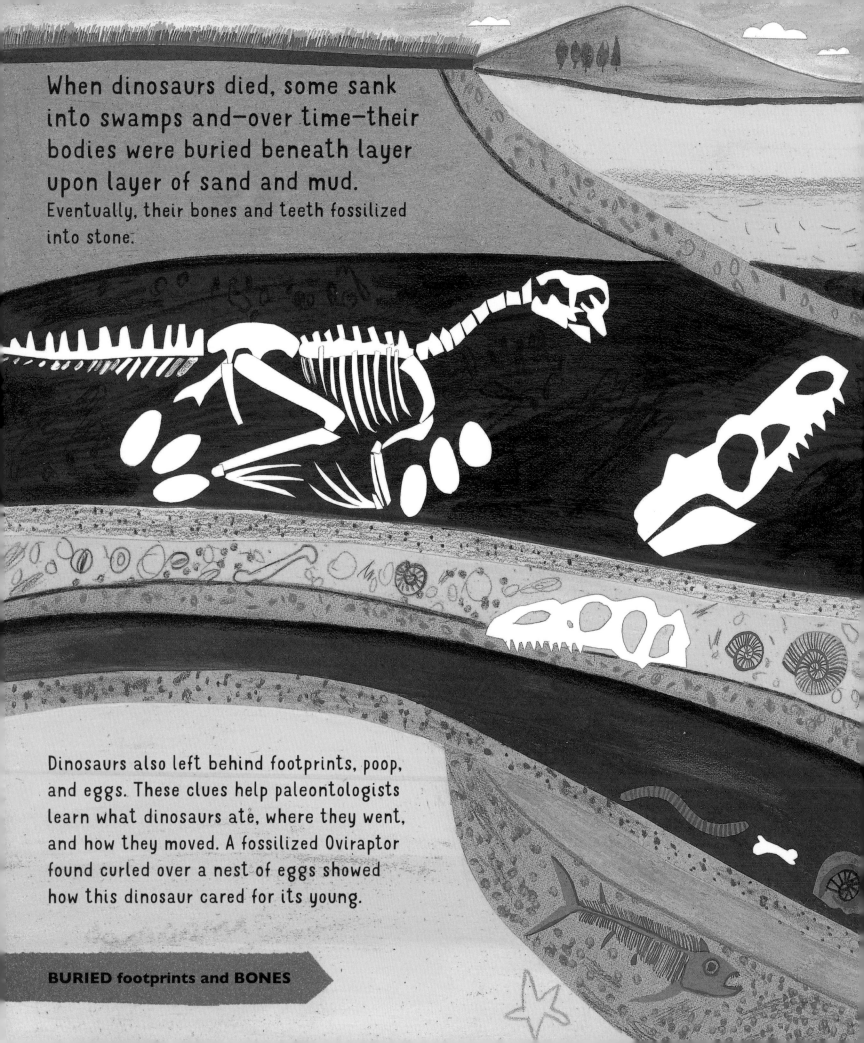

When dinosaurs died, some sank into swamps and—over time—their bodies were buried beneath layer upon layer of sand and mud. Eventually, their bones and teeth fossilized into stone.

Dinosaurs also left behind footprints, poop, and eggs. These clues help paleontologists learn what dinosaurs ate, where they went, and how they moved. A fossilized Oviraptor found curled over a nest of eggs showed how this dinosaur cared for its young.

BURIED footprints and BONES

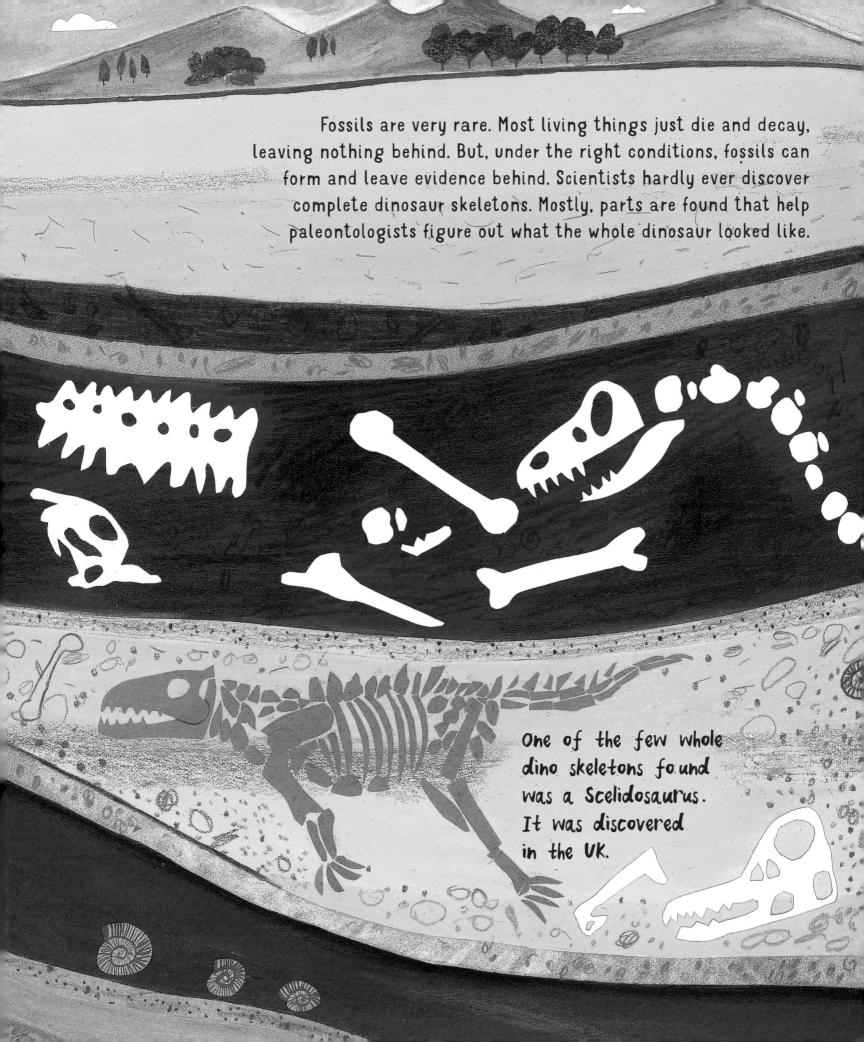

Fossils are very rare. Most living things just die and decay, leaving nothing behind. But, under the right conditions, fossils can form and leave evidence behind. Scientists hardly ever discover complete dinosaur skeletons. Mostly, parts are found that help paleontologists figure out what the whole dinosaur looked like.

One of the few whole dino skeletons found was a Scelidosaurus. It was discovered in the UK.

Fossilized bones are often found by people
who spot them in a piece of rock. Rain, wind, and waves
wear away the landscape over time and reveal fossils that have
been hidden for millions of years. Sometimes a tiny fossil can
lead to the discovery of a huge dinosaur graveyard.

DINOSAUR HUNTERS

From gigantic skulls and leg bones to teeth and trackways, fossils have mystified and wowed dinosaur hunters for hundreds of years. Dinosaur discoveries even led to "Bone Wars" in the late 1800s, when dinosaur hunters set out to destroy each others' finds. This is because they all wanted to be celebrated as the most famous dinosaur hunter.

If you want to go dinosaur hunting today, you can just look outside at a bird! Our modern birds are descendants of two-legged theropod dinosaurs that survived the asteroid strike. They survived because they were small, could eat lots of different things, escape easily, and breed quickly.

For years, scientists were puzzled about where birds came from. The answer lay in fossils which revealed this fascinating evolutionary story.

Birds, in all their spectacular diversity, capture the wonder of the mighty dinosaurs. So when you're next in the park or walking to school, look up into the sky and see how many dinosaur descendants you can spot!

Now, the pace of dinosaur discovery is staggering. Fossils have been found on every continent and new dinosaur species are named almost every week!

Teams of scientists are working together across the world to understand how dinosaurs looked, moved, and even sounded. The discovery of very long nose bones in a Parasaurolophus revealed that it might have made a noise like a trombone!

MODERN-DAY DISCOVERIES

Today, museums are full of people learning about the prehistoric creatures that dominated planet Earth for more than 170 million years. You can be a part of dinosaur discovery too by visiting places where fossils are found. If you're lucky, you might find one and be able to hold a little part of the story of dinosaurs in your hand.

Glossary of useful words

MODERN-DAY DISCOVERIES

BIRDS

Asteroid—a rock that floats in space around the sun.

Biodiversity—all of the different types of living things on Earth.

Continent—massive areas of land separated by water. Earth has seven continents.

Descendants—living things that evolved from other living things.

Ecosystem—all the living and non-living things that exist in one place and their connections with each other.

Evolution—the gradual change of living things over time.

Extinction—when a type of living thing dies out and disappears from Earth forever.

Fossil—evidence in rocks of things that lived millions of years ago.

Greenhouse gases—gases such as carbon dioxide and methane that cause Earth's climate to heat up.

TRIASSIC
51-201 million years ago

JURASSIC early
201-174 million years ago

JURASSIC late
164-145 million years ago

CRETACEOUS
145-66 million years ago

Paleontologist—a scientist who studies fossils.

Pangaea/Gondwana/Laurasia—super-sized land masses on Earth hundreds of millions of years ago.

Predators—animals that hunt and kill other animals.

Sauropods—types of dinosaurs with long necks, long tails, small heads, and four thick legs.

Theropods—includes all the meat-eating dinosaurs which walked on their back legs and had short front legs. Birds are the last remaining theropods.

Trackways—the footprints left behind by animals.

TRIASSIC
5 million years ago

CRETACEOUS
145-66 million years ago

CRETACEOUS
145-66 million years ago

CRETACEOUS
145-66 million years ago

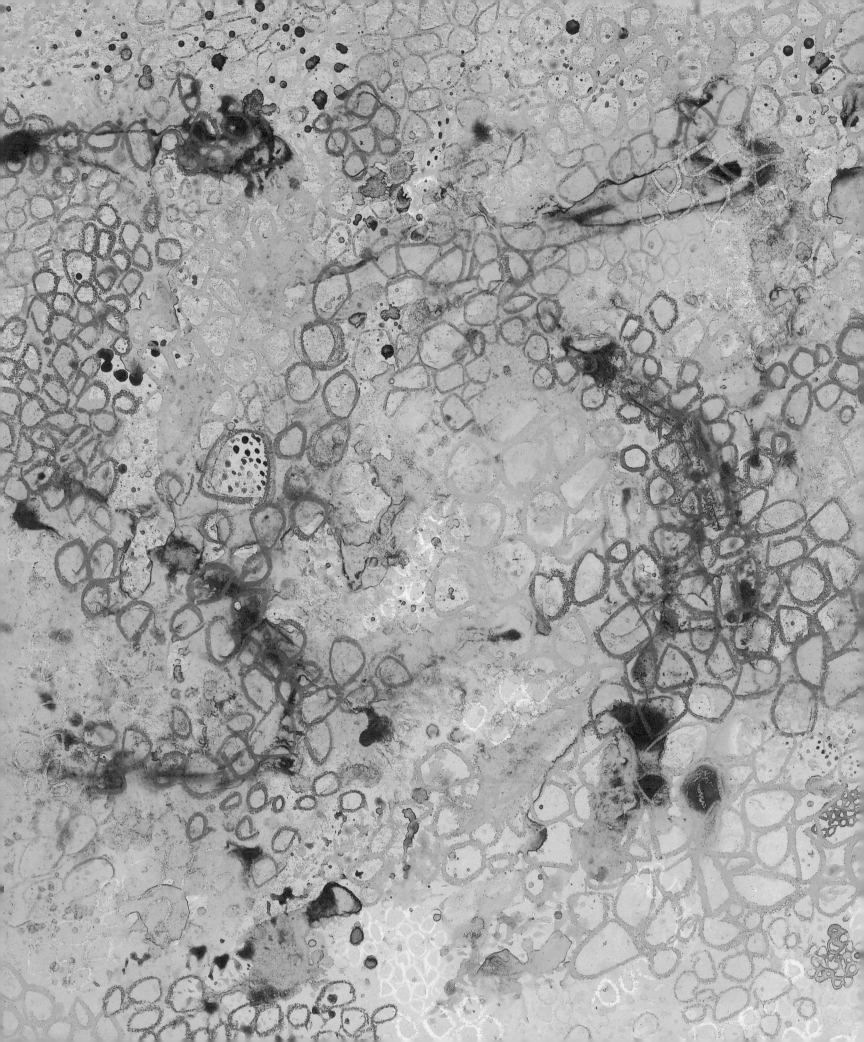